# Invest Like a Pro

## *A Practical Guide to Wealth Management*

# Table of Contents

1. Introduction . . . . . . . . . . . . . . . . . . . . . . . . . . . . 1

2. Understanding Financial Fundamentals . . . . . . . . . . . . 2

    2.1. Basic Concepts in Finance . . . . . . . . . . . . . . . 2

3. Time Value of Money . . . . . . . . . . . . . . . . . . . . . . 3

4. Risk and Return . . . . . . . . . . . . . . . . . . . . . . . . 4

    4.1. The Magic of Compounding . . . . . . . . . . . . . . 4

    4.2. Fundamental Analysis in Investing . . . . . . . . . . 5

5. Financial Statements Analysis . . . . . . . . . . . . . . . . 6

6. Macroeconomic Analysis . . . . . . . . . . . . . . . . . . . 7

    6.1. The Seven Key Investment Principles . . . . . . . . . 7

7. Wealth Creation: A Comprehensive Overview . . . . . . . . 9

    7.1. Understanding Wealth Creation . . . . . . . . . . . . 9

    7.2. The Power of Compound Interest . . . . . . . . . . . 9

    7.3. Creating a Financial Plan . . . . . . . . . . . . . . . 10

    7.4. Cultivating Financial Literacy . . . . . . . . . . . . . 10

    7.5. Diversification of Investments . . . . . . . . . . . . . 11

    7.6. The Role of Risk in Wealth Creation . . . . . . . . . 11

    7.7. Continual Review and Adjustments . . . . . . . . . . 12

8. Asset Allocation Strategies for Wealth Management . . . . 13

    8.1. The Purpose of Asset Allocation . . . . . . . . . . . . 13

    8.2. Framework of an Asset Allocation Strategy . . . . . 13

    8.3. Rebalancing Your Portfolio . . . . . . . . . . . . . . 14

    8.4. Asset Allocation Models . . . . . . . . . . . . . . . . 14

    8.5. Conclusion . . . . . . . . . . . . . . . . . . . . . . . 15

9. Principles of Successful Investing . . . . . . . . . . . . . . 17

    9.1. Understanding Your Investment Goals . . . . . . . . 17

    9.2. Determining Your Risk Tolerance . . . . . . . . . . . 17

    9.3. Diversification: Spreading Your Investments . . . . . 18

9.4. Regularly Review and Rebalance Your Portfolio . . . . . . . . . 18

9.5. Long-Term Investment Strategy . . . . . . . . . . . . . . . . . 19

9.6. Understanding Compounding . . . . . . . . . . . . . . . . . . 19

9.7. Do Your Homework . . . . . . . . . . . . . . . . . . . . . . . 19

9.8. Patience is the Key . . . . . . . . . . . . . . . . . . . . . . . 20

10. Strategies for Retirement Savings . . . . . . . . . . . . . . . . . 21

10.1. Understanding the Time Value of Money . . . . . . . . . . . 21

10.2. Starting Early . . . . . . . . . . . . . . . . . . . . . . . . . . 21

10.3. The Power of Diversification . . . . . . . . . . . . . . . . . . 22

10.4. Utilizing Tax-Advantaged Accounts . . . . . . . . . . . . . . 22

10.5. Investing in Equities . . . . . . . . . . . . . . . . . . . . . . 22

10.6. The Role of Fixed Income Securities . . . . . . . . . . . . . . 22

10.7. Real Estate and Other Tangibles . . . . . . . . . . . . . . . . 23

10.8. Planning for Inflation . . . . . . . . . . . . . . . . . . . . . . 23

10.9. Regular Reviews and Rebalancing . . . . . . . . . . . . . . . 23

10.10. Seeking Professional Advice . . . . . . . . . . . . . . . . . . 23

11. Risk Management in Investing . . . . . . . . . . . . . . . . . . . 25

11.1. Understanding Risk Tolerance . . . . . . . . . . . . . . . . . 25

11.2. Types of Investment Risks . . . . . . . . . . . . . . . . . . . 26

11.3. The Risk-Reward Trade-off . . . . . . . . . . . . . . . . . . . 27

11.4. Risk Management Strategies . . . . . . . . . . . . . . . . . . 27

12. Building a Winning Portfolio . . . . . . . . . . . . . . . . . . . . 29

12.1. Set Your Investment Goals . . . . . . . . . . . . . . . . . . . 29

12.2. Determine Your Risk Tolerance . . . . . . . . . . . . . . . . 29

12.3. Understand Investment Types . . . . . . . . . . . . . . . . . 30

12.4. Time Frame . . . . . . . . . . . . . . . . . . . . . . . . . . . 30

12.5. Diversify Your Investments . . . . . . . . . . . . . . . . . . . 31

12.6. Asset Allocation . . . . . . . . . . . . . . . . . . . . . . . . . 31

12.7. Regular Review and Rebalancing . . . . . . . . . . . . . . . . 31

12.8. Investing in a Down Market . . . . . . . . . . . . . . . . . . . 32

12.9. The Role of a Financial Advisor . . . . . . . . . . . . . . . . . . . . . . . . . . . 32

13. Real Estate as a Wealth-Generating Asset . . . . . . . . . . . . . . . . . . 33

13.1. The Basics of Real Estate Investing . . . . . . . . . . . . . . . . . . . . . 33

13.2. Why Real Estate as a Wealth-Generating Asset? . . . . . . . . . 34

13.3. Building a Real Estate Portfolio . . . . . . . . . . . . . . . . . . . . . . . . 34

13.4. Adding Value to Your Properties . . . . . . . . . . . . . . . . . . . . . . . . 35

13.5. Risk Management in Real Estate Investing . . . . . . . . . . . . . . . 35

13.6. Conclusion of Real Estate as a Wealth-Generating Asset . . . . 36

14. Tax-Advantaged Investing Strategies . . . . . . . . . . . . . . . . . . . . . . 37

14.1. Traditional and Roth Individual Retirement Accounts . . . . . 37

14.2. 401(k) Plans . . . . . . . . . . . . . . . . . . . . . . . . . . . . . . . . . . . . . . . . . 37

14.3. Health Savings Accounts (HSAs) . . . . . . . . . . . . . . . . . . . . . . . 38

14.4. 529 Plan . . . . . . . . . . . . . . . . . . . . . . . . . . . . . . . . . . . . . . . . . . . . . 38

14.5. Tax-Managed Mutual Funds . . . . . . . . . . . . . . . . . . . . . . . . . . . 38

14.6. Municipal Bonds . . . . . . . . . . . . . . . . . . . . . . . . . . . . . . . . . . . . . 39

14.7. Tax-loss Harvesting . . . . . . . . . . . . . . . . . . . . . . . . . . . . . . . . . . . 39

14.8. Gift and Estate Tax Advantages . . . . . . . . . . . . . . . . . . . . . . . . 39

15. Legacy Planning and Wealth Transfer . . . . . . . . . . . . . . . . . . . . . 41

15.1. What Is Legacy Planning? . . . . . . . . . . . . . . . . . . . . . . . . . . . . . 41

15.2. Estate Planning Vs. Legacy Planning . . . . . . . . . . . . . . . . . . . . 41

15.3. The Importance of Wealth Transfer . . . . . . . . . . . . . . . . . . . . . 42

15.4. Optimal Strategies for Wealth Transfer . . . . . . . . . . . . . . . . . . 42

15.5. Charitable Giving . . . . . . . . . . . . . . . . . . . . . . . . . . . . . . . . . . . . . 43

15.6. Concluding Remarks . . . . . . . . . . . . . . . . . . . . . . . . . . . . . . . . . . 44

# Chapter 1. Introduction

Welcome to an exciting journey of financial empowerment! Our Special Report, "Invest Like a Pro: A Practical Guide to Wealth Management," empowers you with the insider know-how to chart your financial future with confidence. We've expertly distilled complex investment strategies applied by world-class wealth managers into everyday language and practical steps you can start applying immediately. Whether you're an experienced investor or stepping onto this path for the first time, you'll find value in our easy-to-follow guide, laced with real-world examples and must-know tips. Dive in and lay the groundwork for the creation, growth, and preservation of your wealth. Start thriving today by making informed and strategic decisions about your financial future!

# Chapter 2. Understanding Financial Fundamentals

Understanding financial fundamentals is akin to building the foundation of a house. Without this essential underpinning, even the most exquisite mansion can crumble, metaphorically translating into unsuccessful investments in the world of finance. Let's tap into the reservoir of financial knowledge that all wise investors must grasp before navigating the labyrinth of investments.

## 2.1. Basic Concepts in Finance

Before we delve into the intricacies of investments, let's get accustomed to some basic concepts in finance.

# Chapter 3. Time Value of Money

Time and money share a profound relationship. $100 today, in most instances, is worth more than $100 a year from now. Why? Because money available today can be invested to generate returns, which adds to its value over time. This is known as the time value of money (TVM). It's important to comprehend TVM because it is fundamental to understanding further financial concepts like net present value, internal rate of return, and bond yields.

# Chapter 4. Risk and Return

Understanding risk and return is instrumental in making sound investment decisions. High-risk investments typically come with the potential for higher returns but also higher chances of losses. Safer investments usually yield lower returns. Here, it's pivotal to understand your risk tolerance, which depends upon factors like your economic situation, age, and individual personality. Balancing risk and return helps in creating a diversified investment portfolio that aligns with your investment goals and risk appetite.

# 4.1. The Magic of Compounding

Often dubbed the 'eight wonder of the world', compound interest is that sprinkle of magic that can transform a small pile of money into a mountain of wealth over time. While simple interest is the interest earned only on the original sum invested, compound interest is earned on the original sum as well as the accumulated interest over time.

Let's illustrate this with an example:

Suppose you invest $10,000 at an annual interest rate of 5%. In the case of simple interest, after 20 years you'll have $20,000, considering no withdrawals in these years. But in the case of compound interest, assuming it's compounded annually, after 20 years you'll have approximately $26,533, again considering no withdrawals. The key here is to start early, reinvest any returns in the same or other investments, and allow your money to snowball over time.

## 4.2. Fundamental Analysis in Investing

An essential tool in an investor's arsenal, fundamental analysis helps you evaluate a security's intrinsic value and analyse the factors that could influence its price in future. This might involve inspecting a company's financial statements, considering macroeconomic indicators like economy's health, industry trends and even geopolitical events.

# Chapter 5. Financial Statements Analysis

Financial statements are akin to a company's report card. Three critical financial statements you should know are:

1. Balance sheet: It gives a snapshot of a company's assets, liabilities, and shareholders' equity at a specific point in time.

2. Income statement: It shows the company's revenues, costs, and expenses over a period, portraying net profit or a loss (bottom line).

3. Cash flow statement: It illustrates where a company's cash came from (cash inflows) and where it went (cash outflows) over a period.

By scrutinising these statements, an investor can deduce a lot about a company's financial health and operational efficiency.

# Chapter 6. Macroeconomic Analysis

A broader perspective needs to be taken when investing. It's crucial to consider the overall health of the economy, inflation rates, job growth, monetary policy, and more. Each of these factors can impact the performance of investments significantly.

## 6.1. The Seven Key Investment Principles

Let's conclude this chapter with seven fundamental investment principles – like your nodes on the investment compass:

1. Start Early: The soonest, the better. It gives your investments more time to grow – thanks to the magic of compounding.

2. Embrace Diversification: Invest in a mix of different securities to spread and minimize risk.

3. Consistently Invest: Regular investments, irrespective of market conditions, pave the way for better returns in the long run.

4. Understand What You Invest In: Conduct thorough research and choose your investments wisely.

5. Be Patient: Investing is a long-term game. Don't panic during market fluctuations.

6. Rebalance Portfolio: Periodic portfolio rebalancing ensures it remains aligned with your financial goals.

7. Keep Emotions at Bay: Make informed decisions based on logic, not sentiments.

Armed with these financial fundamentals, you're now ready to move on to the deeper waters of investing. Remember, investing is a journey, not a destination – so continual learning is your key companion!

# Chapter 7. Wealth Creation: A Comprehensive Overview

The foundation of a stable and prosperous financial future is wealth creation, the process whereby individuals or businesses increase their economic value through the accumulation of assets over time. This journey requires knowledge, strategic planning, and diligent implementation. Nonetheless, even individuals new to investing can navigate this path successfully with the right tools and information.

## 7.1. Understanding Wealth Creation

The primary step on the path to wealth creation is understanding what wealth, indeed, is. Wealth is not merely an accumulation of income; it is built by acquiring assets that appreciate in value over time. These assets can be physical possessions (like property or fine art), financial investments (like stocks, bonds, or mutual funds), and even skills and education that increase an individual's earning potential.

Managing and increasing these wealth-generating assets will ensure you have a head start in achieving your financial goals, whether it is buying a home, securing your retirement, or establishing a financial reserve for potential business opportunities or emergencies.

## 7.2. The Power of Compound Interest

One of the key aspects of wealth creation is understanding the power of compound interest. Often referred to as "interest on interest," compound interest enables your investment to grow exponentially over time as you earn interest not only on your original investment (or principal) but also on the interest you've already earned.

Here's a basic example: Suppose you invest $1,000 at an annual interest rate of 5%, compounded yearly. At the end of the first year, you'll earn $50 in interest, making your total worth $1,050. In the second year, you'll earn 5% on $1,050, equating to $52.50 of interest. Thus, your total worth becomes $1,102.50 and continues growing in this manner.

The key to taking advantage of compound interest is starting early and being patient because the most significant growth happens in the later years.

# 7.3. Creating a Financial Plan

Mapping out your financial goals and the steps needed to achieve them is an integral part of the wealth creation process. A robust financial plan should encompass the following elements:

1. Your financial goals
2. Detailed analysis of your current financial situation
3. Planned saving and investment strategies
4. Risk management and insurance
5. Retirement planning
6. Estate planning

Your financial plan should evolve over time, reflecting changes in your personal circumstances, financial goals, and market conditions.

# 7.4. Cultivating Financial Literacy

Financial literacy provides the knowledge and understanding required to make informed and effective decisions about financial management. Educate yourself about the various investment options available, their associated risks and returns, financial market operations, and the influence of economic indicators on market performance.

Books, online courses, webinars, and financial advisors can all be valuable resources for enhancing your financial knowledge.

# 7.5. Diversification of Investments

Diversification is a risk management strategy that mixes a variety of investments within a portfolio. It can be achieved across asset classes (stocks, bonds, real estate), within asset classes (different industries or regions), and over time (investing at different periods).

By diversifying your investments, you spread risk and, theoretically, ensure that at least some of your assets will perform well, even when others aren't.

# 7.6. The Role of Risk in Wealth Creation

Risk plays an integral role in the wealth creation process. While certain risks can endanger your wealth and need to be managed – such as the risk of financial loss due to an ill-conceived investment – other risks may yield considerable rewards.

Assessing your risk appetite and capacity before investing is crucial. A common strategy is adjusting risk levels according to age – younger investors can afford to take on more risk due to their longer investment horizon, while older investors might opt for more conservative investments.

# 7.7. Continual Review and Adjustments

Your wealth creation journey is a dynamic process that requires regular review and adjustments based on changes in your financial goals, macroeconomic conditions, and personal circumstances. Regular portfolio reviews and rebalancing maintains your desired level of risk and ensures your investments align with your financial objectives.

Wealth creation might seem daunting, especially for novices. However, armed with the right knowledge and tools, anyone can embark on this journey. Remember, the prime time to take steps towards wealth creation starts now, and the rewards are not only monetary. It's not just about having more, but about securing a better, more secure future for yourself and your loved ones. Engaging in wealth creation sets you up for a lifetime of financial empowerment and independence.

# Chapter 8. Asset Allocation Strategies for Wealth Management

Let's start with an overview of what asset allocation means in the world of wealth management. Asset allocation is the process of diversifying investments among different asset classes such as equities, bonds, cash, and sometimes alternatives such as real estate or commodities. The goal is to balance risk and reward by adjusting the percentage of each asset in an investment portfolio according to the individual's risk tolerance, goals, and investment timeline.

## 8.1. The Purpose of Asset Allocation

The main function of asset allocation strategy is to reduce risk and increase chances of earning returns. This is done through diversification. It's about not putting all the eggs in one basket; instead, it's about investing in a variety of assets. In the long run, this strategy helps protect against significant financial losses if one of your investments doesn't perform well. According to modern portfolio theory, diversifying your investments across various asset classes can potentially yield higher returns and pose a lower risk than any single investment or investment category.

## 8.2. Framework of an Asset Allocation Strategy

When building an asset allocation strategy, consider the following components:

1. Risk Tolerance: This is influenced by your financial goals

alongside your psychological comfort level with investment risk. More volatile assets such as stocks offer higher potential returns but also carry higher risk, while less volatile assets such as bonds offer more stability but lower potential returns.

2. Time Horizon: This defines the length of time the investments will remain untouched until they're needed for the set financial objective. A long-term financial goal, such as retirement savings, may lean towards more volatile assets which have the potential for higher return over time.

3. Financial Goals: Each goal might require a different investment strategy. For example, saving for a house down payment might involve a different mix of assets compared to saving for your child's college fund.

# 8.3. Rebalancing Your Portfolio

Over time, some asset classes may outperform others, causing your portfolio to drift from its original asset allocation. That's where rebalancing comes in. This involves readjusting your portfolio back to your planned asset allocation mix. This might seem counterintuitive as it often involves selling high-performing assets and buying low-performing ones. However, it's important to remember that this is a strategy to manage risk rather than maximising returns.

# 8.4. Asset Allocation Models

There are several models to consider when tailoring your asset allocation strategy:

1. Strategic Asset Allocation: This model follows a 'set it and forget it' approach. It establishes and adheres to a base policy mix—a fixed combination of assets based on expected rates of return for each asset class.

2. Tactical Asset Allocation: This model is more flexible. It allows deviations from the basic mix to capitalise on market pricing anomalies or strong forecasted performance from a specific asset class.

3. Insured Asset Allocation: With this approach, the investor sets a baseline value for the portfolio and rebalances when the portfolio's value drops. It helps to ensure the value of the portfolio doesn't fall below a predefined minimum.

4. Integrated Asset Allocation: In this approach, an investor considers both their economic expectations and their risk in establishing an asset mix. It's a blend of all the previous approaches.

5. Dynamic Asset Allocation: In this approach, the investment mix is continuously adjusted based on market and economic indicators.

Remember, every investor is unique and there's no one-size-fits-all model. You should tailor your asset allocation strategy based on your individual financial goals, risk tolerance, and time horizon.

# 8.5. Conclusion

Developing an effective asset allocation strategy is key to successful wealth management. It helps to stabilize your portfolio during turbulent times and set you on the right path to achieving your financial goals. Understanding the risk-reward tradeoff of different asset classes, sticking to your plan, and periodically rebalancing your portfolio are all vital tactics to manage your wealth.

While the content provided herein gives a foundation for optimal asset allocation, we encourage you to seek advice from a financial advisor that takes into account your unique financial circumstances, risk tolerance, and investment objectives. Remember, investing involves risk, including the potential loss of principal, and it's vital to do your research and due diligence before making any investment decisions.

# Chapter 9. Principles of Successful Investing

Successful investing isn't just about picking the next big thing or getting lucky on a hot tip. It's about understanding and practicing important principles day in and day out. These principles provide a solid foundation for managing wealth, making informed decisions, and ensuring longevity of your investments. Let's delve into these principles to gain a solid footing on your investment journey.

## 9.1. Understanding Your Investment Goals

Before you make any investments, it's crucial to define what you hope to achieve with your money. Your goals might include buying a house, saving for retirement, or building an emergency fund. Recognize that each goal may demand a different investment strategy.

For example, if you're saving for retirement and have several decades until you plan to retire, you might choose to invest largely in stocks, which have historically offered higher returns over long periods. If, however, you're saving for a down payment on a house you plan to buy in a couple of years, a safer investment like a savings account or a Certificate of Deposit (CD) could be more suitable.

## 9.2. Determining Your Risk Tolerance

Risk tolerance is the degree of variability in investment returns that you are willing to withstand. If you need your portfolio to stay as close to its original value as possible, you are a risk-averse investor.

On the other hand, if you are comfortable with the possibility of losing money for the potential of higher returns, you have a high-risk tolerance.

It's important to strike the right balance between risk and reward. Taking on too much risk may result in losing money, but being overly conservative can lead to insufficient growth. Our risk tolerance will often dictate how we should allocate our investments among different asset classes.

# 9.3. Diversification: Spreading Your Investments

Diversification is a strategy that can be summed up as "Don't put all your eggs in one basket." It involves spreading your investments around so that your exposure to any one type of asset is limited. This practice is designed to help reduce the volatility of your portfolio over time and optimize returns.

Diversification doesn't guarantee you won't suffer losses, but it can help reduce the impact of any one single investment on your overall portfolio. It's also worth noting that proper diversification involves not only diversifying among different asset classes but also within asset classes.

# 9.4. Regularly Review and Rebalance Your Portfolio

Investments should not be set and forgotten. Regularly reviewing and rebalancing your investment portfolio is essential to remain aligned with your investment goals.

Over time, some investments may perform better than others, causing your portfolio balance to drift from its original asset allocation. You might find that this new allocation doesn't align with your risk tolerance or investment timeline anymore. Hence, periodic rebalancing—selling off outperformers and purchasing underperformers—is necessary to bring the portfolio back into line with your original strategy.

# 9.5. Long-Term Investment Strategy

When faced with market volatility, investors may feel compelled to make short-term decisions that deviate from their investment plan. However, it's important to stick with your long-term investing strategy and avoid reactionary decisions based on temporary market conditions.

Short-term market events are often just noise that can distract from the big picture. By keeping a long-term perspective, you can prevent being swayed by recent market activity, thus allowing your investments time to compound and grow.

# 9.6. Understanding Compounding

Albert Einstein reportedly said compounding is the eighth wonder of the world. Compounding is when the interest that accrues to an amount of money in turn accrues interest itself. It's the process of generating earnings on an asset's reinvested earnings. With time, compounding can produce significant growth in your investments.

# 9.7. Do Your Homework

Before investing in any asset, it's crucial to do thorough research. That might include reading financial news, annual reports, or industry analyses. It could also mean finding a reputable financial advisor who can provide you with expert insight.

Remember, investing without understanding is akin to gambling. Hence, never invest in something you don't understand fully as the implications could be financially devastating.

# 9.8. Patience is the Key

The investment journey is more like a marathon and not a sprint. Often, it's not about making a quick buck, but about staying the course, being patient, and letting the magic of compounding work its wonders over the long run.

In conclusion, investing involves more than just buying and selling stocks. It's about aligning your investments with your goals, understanding the level of risk that you're willing to accept, diversifying your investments, and sticking close to your plan. Laying a solid foundation on these principles will equip you with the resilience and flexibility needed to navigate the financial waters confidently. And remember, the journey to successful investing is exactly that - a journey. A clear understanding, patience, and discipline can make this journey not just successful but rewarding.

# Chapter 10. Strategies for Retirement Savings

Firstly, let's set the stage for understanding retirement savings. Retirement savings are funds that you set aside during your working years to provide an income when you're no longer working. There are various strategies for retirement savings, ranging from simple savings accounts to sophisticated investment portfolios. We'll explore these in detail.

## 10.1. Understanding the Time Value of Money

The first key concept in retirement saving is understanding the time value of money. Simply put, this is the idea that money available today is worth more than the same amount in the future. This is because the money can be invested and earn interest, so therefore, the longer your money can be invested, the more it can grow. Harnessing the time value of money through compound interest (earning interest on interest) is the first major step towards building a retirement nest egg.

## 10.2. Starting Early

Piggybacking on the concept of time value, the second strategy is to start saving for retirement as early as possible. The sooner you start setting money aside, the more time it has to accrue interest and grow. Starting to save in your 20s as opposed to your 40s can make a drastic difference in the total sum accumulated by the time you retire, assuming the same amount is set aside each year.

## 10.3. The Power of Diversification

Next, diversification plays a crucial role in any retirement saving strategy. Spreading your investments across a wide variety of assets and sectors provides a cushion as the overall risk is spread. If one sector or asset class performs poorly, others may perform better, balancing out any losses. This also enables you to take advantage of different market cycles, with sectors often moving in opposing directions.

## 10.4. Utilizing Tax-Advantaged Accounts

Tax-advantaged accounts can significantly boost your retirement savings. Depending on your jurisdiction, this might include individual retirement accounts (IRAs), 401(k)s or similar pension plans. These accounts provide either upfront tax deductions, tax-free growth, tax-free withdrawals or a combination of these.

## 10.5. Investing in Equities

Investing a portion of your retirement savings in equities (stocks) is a powerful way to increase your retirement savings due to their potential for high returns. However, equities also carry higher risks than most other investment types.

## 10.6. The Role of Fixed Income Securities

Fixed income securities, such as bonds, play an essential role in providing stable, albeit lower, returns. As you approach retirement, fixed income securities should form an increasingly large portion of your portfolio to preserve capital and provide income.

## 10.7. Real Estate and Other Tangibles

Real estate and other tangible assets can also play a role in a well-rounded retirement savings plan. These investments offset some of the volatility of financial markets and provide a potential hedge against inflation. They also add another level of diversification.

## 10.8. Planning for Inflation

Inflation is a reality that individuals saving for retirement cannot ignore. As inflation increases, the purchasing power of your saved dollars decreases. This is why it's essential to invest in assets that can potentially outpace inflation.

## 10.9. Regular Reviews and Rebalancing

Regularly reviewing and rebalancing your portfolio is crucial to ensure your investments remain aligned with your retirement goals. There's no set frequency for how often this needs to be done – it's dependent on your individual circumstances and preferences. However, a good rule of thumb is at least annually.

## 10.10. Seeking Professional Advice

Finally, as your savings grow, professional advice can help refine your investment strategy and navigate more complex scenarios. A financial advisor can provide personalized advice tailored to your unique circumstances and goals.

To summarize, a successful retirement savings strategy leverages the power of time and compound, diversification, tax-advantaged accounts, the potential of equities, the stability of fixed income securities, the tangibility of real estate, the protection against inflation, regular portfolio reviews, and professional advice. By carefully considering each of these elements and integrating them into your plan, you can create a powerful retirement savings strategy designed to deliver a secure and comfortable retirement.

# Chapter 11. Risk Management in Investing

Understanding risk and managing it effectively is a key aspect of successful investing. You could have the perfect investment plan, but if you don't handle the associated risks, you could end up losing a significant amount of your wealth. Risk, in an investment context, refers to the uncertainty of returns. In this chapter, we are going to delve deeper into risk management in investing, talking about risk tolerance, different types of risk, risk-reward trade-off, and strategies for managing risk.

## 11.1. Understanding Risk Tolerance

Risk tolerance refers to the amount of risk an investor is comfortable taking, or the degree of uncertainty an investor is able to handle. It varies from one individual to another due to several factors such as age, financial capabilities, income, and personal beliefs. For example, a young investor might typically have a higher risk tolerance because they have a longer investment horizon and more time to recover losses.

However, risk tolerance is not a constant factor. It can change as your life situation evolves. It is therefore essential to reassess your risk tolerance periodically, especially after significant life events such as inheritance, marriage, birth of a child, or retirement.

So how can you determine your risk tolerance? Typically, wealth managers or financial advisors use questionnaires to assess this. They will take into account your financial situation, investment goals, and your emotional capacity to handle the potential of loss. Answering these questions as honestly as possible is vital to understanding your risk tolerance accurately.

# 11.2. Types of Investment Risks

To manage risk effectively, one must first understand the different types of risks involved in investing. Here are some of the most common:

1. **Market Risk**: This is the risk of an investment losing its value due to various economic events that can affect the entire market. Market risks include interest rate risk, inflation risk, currency risk, and many more.

2. **Liquidity Risk**: Liquidity refers to how quickly an investment can be sold without affecting its price. Liquidity risk occurs when there is difficulty in selling an investment quickly without cutting its price significantly.

3. **Credit Risk**: This is the risk of a corporate or government default on a debt that has affected the bondholders' return.

4. **Operational Risk**: This risk arises from failures in a company's day-to-day operations. It could be caused by breakdowns in a company's procedures, systems, or policies.

Now that you know the types of risks, it is also essential to understand that they can either be systematic or unsystematic. Systematic risk refers to the risk that affects all securities equally, and it can't be eliminated or reduced through diversification. Unsystematic risk, on the other hand, can be reduced by diversification as it impacts a specific industry or a particular company.

One of the primary roles of a wealth manager, or you as an individual investor, is to identify these risks and take steps to mitigate their impact. Next, let's see how you can mitigate these risks.

# 11.3. The Risk-Reward Trade-off

Every investment carries a certain degree of risk and potential return; this is known as the risk-reward trade-off. As an investor, you must understand that the potential for higher rewards comes with higher risk. Thus, aligning your investments with your risk tolerance is vital. While an aggressive investor might be comfortable with high-risk, high-reward investments, a conservative investor might prefer lower-risk investments that offer steady but modest returns.

When it comes to this trade-off, diversification is a strategy often advocated by wealth managers. By spreading your investments across a variety of assets, you can mitigate the risk associated with any one investment. This strategy acts as a safety net because the positive performance of some assets can minimize the detrimental performance of others, leading to a balanced and less risky overall portfolio.

# 11.4. Risk Management Strategies

Lastly, let's look at some strategies you can use to manage your investment risks:

1. **Diversification**: As mentioned earlier, this involves allocating your investments across various assets to minimize the impact of any single investment's poor performance.

2. **Asset Allocation**: This refers to how an investment portfolio is divided among the different kinds of investment assets, like stocks, bonds, and cash.

3. **Hedging**: This refers to making an investment to reduce the risk of adverse price movements in an asset. Often, it involves using complex financial instruments known as derivatives.

4. **Insurance**: Insurance is another way to manage risk, especially for significant investments or assets. It can protect you from

catastrophic losses.

5. **Regular Portfolio Review**: Successful risk management necessitates regular portfolio reviews. This will help identify any potential risks that might have crept up and make necessary adjustments.

6. **Seek Professional Advice**: If you're unsure, it's always intelligent to seek professional advice. Financial advisors or wealth managers can provide helpful insights based on their experience and expertise.

Risk management may seem like a daunting aspect of investing, but once well understood and implemented, it serves as your protective shield against potential losses. Through meticulous planning and strategic decisions, you can navigate through the risky waters of investing, ensuring not just your financial well-being but also peace of mind.

# Chapter 12. Building a Winning Portfolio

Understanding your investment goals, risk tolerance, and time frame are the first steps in crafting a winning portfolio. Investing is not simply about choosing a collection of assets, but it's crafting a holistic strategy, designed to achieve your financial objectives while effectively managing risk. In this chapter, we will show you how to build your winning portfolio, step by step.

Before we get started, remember: investing should never be a gamble - you don't have to risk everything to gain something.

## 12.1. Set Your Investment Goals

The starting point of any investment strategy should be defining your goals. Why are you investing? What do you want your money to achieve? Common goals include wealth accumulation, retirement planning, buying a house, funding higher education, or simply beating inflation.

By setting investment goals, you have a target to aim for, making it easier to plan, monitor progress, and stay motivated on your investing journey.

## 12.2. Determine Your Risk Tolerance

Risk tolerance is your ability and willingness to lose some or all of your original investment in exchange for greater potential returns. Are you a conservative investor who prefers to keep risks to a minimum, or are you an aggressive investor willing to endure greater market swings for potentially higher returns? Your risk tolerance is influenced by factors such as your financial capacity, investment horizon, and personal disposition towards risk.

Identify your risk tolerance to select suitable investment products. A portfolio that generates discomfort, insecurity, or sleepless nights, regardless of potential gains, isn't a winning one.

# 12.3. Understand Investment Types

There's a plethora of financial assets available, each offering different levels of risk and return:

1. Stocks: Equity stakes in a company. Stocks can deliver substantial profits, but they also carry significant risks.

2. Bonds: Loans to a corporate or government entity. They provide lower returns than stocks but are less risky.

3. Mutual Funds: A diversified mix of stocks, bonds, and other assets managed by investment professionals.

4. Exchange-Traded Funds (ETFs): Like mutual funds but can be traded like stocks.

5. Certificates of Deposit: Time-defined deposits with a bank. They provide a guaranteed return but low interest.

6. Real Estate: Physical property. Real estate can provide income and potential appreciation but involves more hands-on work.

Choosing the right mix of these investments is key to constructing a winning portfolio.

# 12.4. Time Frame

Your investment horizon is another crucial factor. Short-term goals might warrant a conservative approach, while long-term goals like retirement saving might entail more aggressive investments, given the longer time to recover from potential losses.

# 12.5. Diversify Your Investments

Diversification involves spreading your investments across various assets and asset classes to mitigate risk. It's about creating a mix of investments that collectively perform well, even if some individual assets underperform.

Ensuring your portfolio holds both domestic and international assets can also provide diversification benefits.

# 12.6. Asset Allocation

Your investment strategy hinges on how you allocate your assets. Asset allocation can influence over 90% of portfolio performance, making it arguably the most crucial part of building a winning portfolio.

Even within broader asset classes of stocks, bonds, and cash equivalents, allocation should be further diversified. For instance, within equities, investments can be spread between different sectors, market capitalizations, and geography.

Asset allocation should align with your risk tolerance, time frame, and investment goals.

# 12.7. Regular Review and Rebalancing

Regularly reviewing and rebalancing your portfolio is fundamental to ensure it stays aligned with your goals. Over time, certain investments might perform better than others, causing your portfolio to deviate from your initial asset allocation.

Rebalancing involves realigning your portfolio back to your original asset allocation by selling over-performing assets and buying under-performing ones. This exercise not only maintains the risk-return balance but also institutionalizes the "buy low, sell high" principle.

# 12.8. Investing in a Down Market

During market downturns, instinct might compel you to sell and cut losses. However, down markets can present excellent buying opportunities for the wise investor. Remember the age-old wisdom of buying low and selling high.

Seeing your portfolio's value diminish can be challenging, but a well-diversified portfolio aligned to your long-term goals should weather short-term market fluctuations.

# 12.9. The Role of a Financial Advisor

Although it's entirely feasible to manage your portfolio independently, the benefits of a trusted financial advisor can be invaluable. They provide objective advice, help navigate complex financial markets, and offer disciplined investing approaches, especially during market turbulence.

In conclusion, building a winning portfolio is an art combining science, intuition, resolve, and discipline. Establish your goals, align them with your risk tolerance, and custom design your portfolio to fit your needs and aspirations. Remember, investing is a marathon, not a sprint. So, focus on long-term strategy than short-lived market trends, because, in the steady pursuit of your financial goals, great wealth can be built.

# Chapter 13. Real Estate as a Wealth-Generating Asset

Real estate, commonly acknowledged as one of the oldest forms of investing, entails the purchase, ownership, management, rental, and/or sale of real estate for profit. Over centuries, it has proven to be a reliable avenue for wealth creation and preservation, demonstrating relative stability, attractive returns, and several other unique benefits that set it apart from other asset classes.

## 13.1. The Basics of Real Estate Investing

An understanding of the fundamental principles underpinning real estate investment is crucial to successfully leveraging it as a wealth-generating asset.

As a form of 'real asset', real estate can either be residential (homes and flats, for example) or commercial (such as office buildings and shopping centers). Investing in real estate can thus be carried out through either purchasing a physical property or buying shares in a real estate investment trust (REIT).

The key tenants of real estate investment include:

1. Return on investment: This is typically derived from rental income and capital appreciation.

2. Leverage: By using a mortgage to finance part of your investment, you're enabled to buy a more expensive property than you could otherwise afford.

3. Capital preservation: Due to its tangibility and enduring demand, real estate often maintains its value over time, even in times of

economic turbulence.

Properties are primarily valued according to their location and the income they generate - this means that the more popular the area and the higher the rental income of a property, the more valuable it typically is.

# 13.2. Why Real Estate as a Wealth-Generating Asset?

There are several reasons why real estate is a compelling wealth-generating asset.

1. Cash flow: The regular income derived from rental properties, after offsetting expenses, provides a constant cash flow, which often increases over time as rents go up and mortgage payments stay the same.

2. Appreciation: The increase in the property's value over time provides a powerful wealth creation tool.

3. Leverage: Real estate allows efficient use of credit, as a large amount of the purchase price can be borrowed.

4. Tax advantages: In many countries, various tax benefits exist for real estate investments such as tax deductions on mortgage interest, operating expenses and costs, and property taxes.

5. Inflation hedge: The value of real estate traditionally increases faster than the rate of inflation over the long term, providing a degree of protection against the erosion of purchasing power.

# 13.3. Building a Real Estate Portfolio

Just like with other investments, diversification is key in real estate. A diverse property portfolio can consist of residential, commercial, and industrial properties, across different locations. Diversification can be achieved by investing in different property types and sectors all while spreading the investments geographically.

It's also worth considering REITs, which invest in commercial real estate, such as office buildings, shopping malls, apartments, and hotels. They offer a way for individual investors to gain exposure to real estate without the need to buy or manage properties themselves.

Start by defining your investment goals, financial capacity, risk tolerance, and time horizon. Once these are clear, you can then establish your investment strategy and start identifying potential properties or REITs that fit your criteria.

# 13.4. Adding Value to Your Properties

Over the short to medium term, property investors can add value to their properties to maximize rental income and potential selling prices. Some common ways to add value include:

1. Renovations
2. Extensions
3. Conversions (for example, turning a large house into multiple flats)

Before undertaking any value-add activity, it's important to ensure that the potential increased income or sale price justifies the cost and time of the work to be done.

# 13.5. Risk Management in Real Estate Investing

Like any investment, real estate does carry risks. Some of the key risks include:

1. Property market downturns

2. Vacancy periods

3. Unexpected maintenance costs

4. Bad tenants

To manage these risks, due diligence is crucial before any investment decision. This means researching the property, the local area, and potentially enlisting professional services such as property inspections and legal advice.

Having a diverse property portfolio, maintaining an emergency fund, and having appropriate insurance in place can also help manage these risks.

# 13.6. Conclusion of Real Estate as a Wealth-Generating Asset

In sum, real estate represents a potent tool in one's investing arsenal, providing a source of stable income, beneficial tax implications, a hedge against inflation, and opportunities to leverage. Coupled with its potential for appreciative value and ability to diversify an investor's portfolio, it remains an avenue of wealth generation that is both accessible and immensely rewarding if approached strategically.

Managed effectively, property can be a godsend for wealth accumulation and preservation, a testament to the enduring relevance of the adage, "Safe as houses."

# Chapter 14. Tax-Advantaged Investing Strategies

Tax-advantaged investing strategies are tools designed by the government to encourage investing and saving by providing tax benefits. They can significantly boost your investment returns over time, especially when coupled with long term investing strategies. In this chapter, we unravel compelling strategies that will help you optimize your finances by leveraging tax regulations and benefits to your advantage.

## 14.1. Traditional and Roth Individual Retirement Accounts

Individual Retirement Accounts (IRA) are a significant component of your long-term savings effort with two main types, Traditional and Roth. The primary distinction between the two is when you pay income taxes.

With Traditional IRAs, you make contributions with pre-taxed income, lowering your current taxable income. Consequently, you pay taxes when you withdraw funds in retirement. It's essential to note that withdrawals before age 59.5 will incur a 10% early withdrawal fee. On the other hand, Roth IRAs use already taxed income for contributions, and withdrawals in retirement are then tax-free, given certain conditions.

## 14.2. 401(k) Plans

A 401(k) is another type of tax-advantaged retirement account, usually sponsored by an employer. Contributions are made pre-tax, lowering your current income subject to taxes. Besides, employers often match a portion of their employee's contributions. However, taxes are deducted during withdrawal in retirement. Again, withdrawals before age 59.5 are penalized.

Similar to an IRA, there's also a Roth 401(k): contributions are post-tax, meaning you pay the tax now so that your withdrawals during retirement are tax-free.

## 14.3. Health Savings Accounts (HSAs)

Health Savings Accounts are an overlooked tax-advantaged investment vehicle. Individuals with high-deductible healthcare plans are eligible to invest in HSAs. The contributions to an HSA are tax-deductible, the growth is tax-free, and if used for eligible medical expenses, the withdrawals are also tax-free. If you stay healthy, your HSA can be a sizeable tax-free investment.

## 14.4. 529 Plan

The 529 Plan is a tax-advantaged savings plan aimed at encouraging savings for future education costs. They are sponsored by states, state agencies, or educational institutions. The plan's main perk is that the withdrawals, including the profits, are tax-free when used for eligible education expenses.

## 14.5. Tax-Managed Mutual Funds

If you invest in mutual funds, considering tax-managed mutual funds could be beneficial. These funds aim to limit the amount of taxable income they distribute to their shareholders using strategies like index tracking, low turnover, and strategic selling.

## 14.6. Municipal Bonds

Municipal bonds offer interest payments that are often free of federal income tax and can be free of state and local taxes if issued within your resident state. These bonds are issued by cities, counties, and states to fund public projects, which provide the tax advantage. Despite the lower interest rate than comparable taxable bonds, the tax advantages can result in a higher yield for investors in higher tax brackets.

## 14.7. Tax-loss Harvesting

Tax-loss harvesting is an underutilized strategy by which you can use investment losses to offset investment gains in order to limit a portion of your tax liability. This strategy can be complex and does require planning and timing, but can be an effective tool for sophisticated investors with the help and advice of a tax professional.

## 14.8. Gift and Estate Tax Advantages

If your investment portfolio is considerable, you're likely to face estate taxes. However, there are strategies to limit the tax burden. For instance, gifting during your lifetime can help deplete your future taxable estate. In 2021, the gift-tax exemption is $15,000 per individual recipient or $30,000 for married couples. Additionally, trusts may be set up which allow for tax-free growth and tax-free distribution depending on the type of trust and jurisdiction.

Each tax-advantaged strategy has its specifics and often requires careful consideration and planning. Keep in mind, tax laws are complex and may change over time, so it's recommended to work with a knowledgeable tax advisor or financial planner to craft the best approach for your circumstances.

Understanding and expertly incorporating tax-advantaged investing strategies into your wealth management plan could have a profound impact on your financial health, letting you keep more of your money and potentially propelling you to attain your financial objectives faster. It is the practical embodiment of working smarter, not harder, when securing your financial future.

# Chapter 15. Legacy Planning and Wealth Transfer

In the realm of wealth management, legacy planning and wealth transfer is a critical piece of the puzzle. While the immediate focus might be on building and growing wealth, it's equally important to think about how that wealth will be passed on. Regardless of the size of your estate, it's prudent to have a solid plan to ensure that your wealth continues to serve your family and your values even after your lifetime.

## 15.1. What Is Legacy Planning?

Legacy planning is a comprehensive approach to estate management. It involves more than just making a will. It includes life insurance, estate planning, wealth transfer, and potentially establishing your legacy through philanthropic efforts. Legacy planning is about fostering a smooth transition of your wealth and assets, with minimal taxes and maximum benefit to your designated beneficiaries.

Influenced by the specific family dynamics, your values, and your financial situation, legacy planning is a custom-built approach, highly specific to you. The aim is not just the transfer of material wealth, but also immaterial wealth, like your values, life lessons, and family customs, which are as essential as your financial assets to your succeeding generations.

## 15.2. Estate Planning Vs. Legacy Planning

While estate planning and legacy planning may sound synonymous, they are distinctly different. Estate planning is focused on the management and disposal of an individual's estate during life and after death. On the other hand, legacy planning is a more holistic process that includes not only the financial assets but also intangible principles and traditions that an individual wishes to pass on.

With legacy planning, you instill a broader perspective, investing your wealth not only in your successors but also in serving social, cultural, or familial causes close to your heart. This could include establishing a charitable trust, creating a family scholarship, or even preserving a historic property. Legacy planning helps you weave your life's work and achievements into a living legacy.

# 15.3. The Importance of Wealth Transfer

Being strategic about wealth transfer is paramount in legacy planning. Unfortunately, a surprising number of wealthy individuals do not have adequate wealth transmission plans in place. Without a proper plan, your hard-earned wealth can be quickly eroded by legal fees, taxes, or family disputes.

Wealth transfer involves planning for the transfer of responsibilities, assets, and wealth onto the next generation in a way that aligns with your desires, minimizes tax implications, and avoids potential disagreements within your successors.

# 15.4. Optimal Strategies for Wealth Transfer

| | |
|---|---|
| Trusts | **Trusts are an incredibly flexible tool to manage and transfer your wealth. A trust fund could hold cash, investments, real estate, and other assets. Placing assets in a trust can provide control over how the assets are distributed, provide potential tax advantages, and protect against creditors.** |
| Family Limited Partnerships or Family Limited Liability Companies | These can also be valuable tools for centralizing family business or investment accounts while providing liability protection and various tax benefits. |
| Life Insurance | Life insurance is a commonly used tool in wealth transfer planning, primarily because its proceeds are usually tax-free to the beneficiary. It can be part of a larger strategy, for instance, to provide for family members, pay estate taxes, or fund a buy-sell agreement for a family business. |

# 15.5. Charitable Giving

Philanthropy can play a pivotal role in shaping your legacy. Charitable giving can help you pass on not only your wealth but your values, and at the same time, avail substantial tax benefits.

Donor-advised funds and private foundations are some of the tools for planning your philanthropic endeavors. These tools allow you to make a charitable contribution, receive an immediate tax benefit, and then recommend donations from the fund over time.

# 15.6. Concluding Remarks

Legacy planning and wealth transfer are sophisticated processes that require thoughtful and strategic planning. Disclosing your wealth transfer plans to your successors can lead to a much smoother wealth transition. And remember, legacy planning is not a one-time event; it is a dynamic process that should evolve with your life, family situation, and changes in law. Working with experienced attorneys, financial advisors, and tax professionals can provide you with the necessary guidance to create a robust plan that can endure through time and legislation changes, ensuring your legacy is preserved and cherished just as you dreamed.